Marketing and Selling to Business Owners

Marketing and Selling to Business Owners

A Financial Advisor's Guide to Dominating this Lucrative Market

by
Robert McLaughlin

2014

© 2014 Robert McLaughlin / Morphic Press. All rights reserved.

No part of this book may be reproduced or transmitted in any form or by any means, electronic or mechanical, without written permission from the author, except for the use of brief quotations in a review.

This book is not meant to be legal, accounting, investment, or financial planning advice. Before taking any actions discussed herein, you should (must!) discuss your plans with your compliance officer and any other relevant professional.

Please note that where I recommend a particular product, such as books from Amazon, I provide a link to the product if possible, such as in the Kindle version of this book. In some cases, if you buy the product by using my link, I will receive a commission through Amazon's "Associate" program. It does not increase the price that you pay, and the fact that I may receive a commission from the sale does not influence my recommendation. I've read all of these books or have listened to the audio versions and have found them to be valuable resources.

First edition: January 2014

ISBN-13: 978-1494886592

ISBN-10: 1494886596

DEDICATION

For my family and friends. Without them, this effort would neither be possible, nor worthwhile.

ADDE PARVUM PARVO
MAGNUS ACERVUS ERIT

(Add a little to a little
and there will be a great heap.)

— Ovid

CONTENTS

Dedication		v
Contents		ix
Preface		xiii
1	**Introduction**	1

I   Set Meaningful Goals   3

2	**Setting Goals**		5
	2.1	What Is a "Goal"?	5
		Specific	5
		Measurable	5
		Attainable	6
		Realistic	6
		Time-targeted	6
	2.2	A Practical Method of Setting Goals	6
		Method 1: Personal Goals Determine Business Goals	7
		Method 2: The "Survival Method"	9
	2.3	Income Goals Determine Daily Activity	9
	2.4	Setting the Numbers–Cold Calling	10
		Calling Hours per Week	10
		Cold Calls per Hour	11
		Percentage of Calls That Become "Contacts"	11
		Percentage of Contacts That Set an Appointment	12
		Percentage of Appointments That Open Accounts	12

		Account Size	13
		Account Revenue Rate	13
		Motivate Yourself	16
	2.5	Other Prospecting Methods	17
		Seminars	17
		Networking	20
		Notes on "Mining your Client List"	20

3 Confidence and Attitude   23

II Choosing a Niche   25

4 Notes on "Natural Markets"   27

5 Business Owners as a Niche   29
	5.1	The Demographics of Business Owners	29
	5.2	Business Owners' Needs	30
	5.3	Finding Business Owners	32
		How Many Prospects?	33
		Not Enough Widget Manufacturers?	34
		Buying a List	34
		Larkspur and JDA	35
		Larkspur	36
		JDA	37
		Cleaning the Larkspur (and JDA) Data	38
		Dun & Bradstreet Lists	40
	5.4	Data Mining	42
	5.5	Prospecting Business Owners	43
		Qualifying Business Owners	44

III Become a Prospecting Machine   47

6 Building a Team   49

CONTENTS xi

7 The Appointment **51**
- 7.1 Don't Work for Free 51
- 7.2 Before the Appointment 52
  - Dealing with the "Gate Keeper" 53
  - Prepare a "Universal Pitch Book" 54
- 7.3 During the Appointment 55
- 7.4 After the Appointment 56

8 Time Management → Success **59**
- 8.1 An Illustrative Tale 59
- 8.2 Scheduling and Chunking 61
- 8.3 Managing Appointments 61
- 8.4 Productivity Tips 63
  - In the Mornings 63
  - Lunchtime 63
  - Shutting Down for the Evening 64
  - General Productivity Tips 64

Appendices **67**

The FA's Business Plan Template **69**

Additional Resources **71**
- General Marketing and Selling 71
- Networking 71
- Cold-Calling 71
- Seminars 72
- Goals and Motivation 72
- Time Management 72
- Learning about Businesses 73

PREFACE

ANOTHER book telling financial advisors how to build their businesses? Do we really need that? Yes, and I'll tell you why. In short, it fills a crucial gap in practically every FA's training. This gap sets up the FA for, at best, significant floundering and increased work, and at worst, for failure.

When I began as an FA I went through the training program at one of the largest and most prestigious (at least then) wire houses. The wire house provided an excellent foundation of technical and investment skills.

However, there was a lack of business training–no discussion of what markets are lucrative, how to create a marketing strategy, and what daily action is needed to build a successful business, and perhaps most importantly how to hit the ground running. As an FA, you can't give good advice to clients if you don't have clients, and you have to make enough money to survive, and that means you have to treat your practice as a business, just like every other successful professional in the country. In the training program, we received little practical advice on how to run a professional practice, or how to build a client base (other than basic sales training).

The author of one prominent book (that's pushed on many advisors) confuses "market" and "method." For example, he claims that networking is a market. It's not. Rather, it's a method to allow you to penetrate a market. The group with whom you network–that is the market. Pick any market, any demographic group. You can network within that market. You can cold call that market. And you can offer seminars to that market. So I found that even some of the "best-sellers" have some gaps.

When I was in my old firm's training program, I filled in that training gap by reading practically every book available on "How To Build a Freakishly Awesome Practice as a Financial Advisor and Make a Fortune Doing It." (No, that's not an actual title, but if you've browsed the "shelves" at Amazon, you know what I mean.) Many of the books are only useful if you have a practice already. For example, they'll teach you how to turn a 250k practice into a million dollar practice. But you need to get to the 250k level first. Many others were too theoretical. Some were pure motivation and platitudes. That's okay because we all need motivation and attitude adjustment now and again.

This book will help FAs in two different situations: (i) new FAs (the "rookies," "newbies," or whatever initials your firm assigns to you); and (ii) FAs who have hit a plateau, are in a lull, or otherwise need to re-energize their marketing so they can focus (like that clichéd "laser beam") on growing their client bases. If you haven't "gone into production" yet, then all the better. Follow the planning steps in this book and, as soon as your firm clears you to start selling, you'll be ready. Even if, however, you're already in production but need some help focusing on a day-to-day method of building business, this book will help you, too. Perhaps it is even more important in the latter situation because the clock is already ticking. You can't waste time.

In my old training program, before we could go into production we had to create a business plan. I was told that most rookies' business plans are either "long on strategy and short on tactics," or the exact opposite. Either one can kill your career as an FA (at least at that firm). You need both strategy and tactics. Strategy gives you the long-term objectives but tactics provide the individual steps necessary. You may have heard the phrase "by the yard it's hard but by the inch it's a cinch." Strategies help you with the "yards" but tactics give you the "inches" because they tell you exactly what you need to do immediately and in every step of the marketing and selling processes. With this book, my goal is for you, through a few simple exercises, to put yourself in a position where you can start confidently selling on your very first day of production.

This book helps you:

1. Decide which lucrative market(s) to target.
2. Create a strategy to market and sell to your chosen markets.
3. Market to a particular niche in an efficient manner.
4. Formulate tactics to give you a step-by-step action plan to achieve your goals.
5. Create a business plan and marketing plan to help you hit your revenue goals.
6. Spend more of your time doing the one thing that is crucial to your success as an FA: selling.

I intend this book to fill in the training gap. I don't believe in a lot of fluff, so I'm only going to "get theoretical" when it's important to understanding why I'm telling you to do a particular thing. Being a "nuts and bolts" kind of person, I like plans, the simpler the better, and checklists, step-by-step processes that don't require a lot of thought. That's not to say that I don't analyze. Believe me, I do. But I don't want you to make the mistake of falling into "analysis paralysis." I've seen that kill many budding FAs' careers.

Here is my advice to you. Quickly skim the entire book. Then go back and do the exercises as you read the book again in greater detail. On your third pass through the book, you'll create your own detailed business plan and you'll be ready to hit the ground running. Some of the exercises require a little thought, but don't make the common mistake of sliding into analysis paralysis. If you get stuck on setting your personal financial goals, make an educated guess and move on to the next step. You should revise your goals yearly, anyway. The key is to keep moving. Think of an FA being like a shark; just as a shark must continue to move forward or it will suffocate and die, an FA must always move forward by prospecting. So let's get moving!

CHAPTER 1

INTRODUCTION

THERE may be no bigger decision you have to make than this: What market do I prospect? Let me emphasize this. Perhaps no other decision you make today will have a greater effect on you throughout your career. Now that I've raised your anxiety level and made you want to avoid making that decision, I'll tell you the key. Just pick one. Rich people? Well duh, but that's not a market. It's not specific enough. There are plenty of markets out there.

As a finanical advisor, you want to acquire and retain lucrative clients. Of all the attractive market niches from which you can choose, this book focuses on one group–business owners. My other books in this series investigate and strategize targeting other lucrative niches. Before discussing business owners in depth, let's look at what exactly is a market. Lawyers? That's a market, too. As is every profession: doctors, CPAs, architects, engineers, etc. I knew one successful advisor marketed only former workers of one particular steel plant. The good news is that there are plenty of people with money. The bad news is that there are almost just as many advisors! But back to my point. Just pick a good market, get into that market and stick with it.

If you love sailing, or golf, for example, you can build a market around that activity. It helps if your passion is one that attracts the wealthy. The coolest thing about building your business around your passion is that people within that circle will necessarily share that passion and that will make your job significantly more enjoyable. Each occupation has a unique set of specific client needs. For example, high salaried professionals need more tax advice than others. The tax code discriminates against high-earning professionals when it comes to retirement planning. Don't laugh–think about it. Learn that story and you'll have a great elevator speech.

Pick a market you like to talk about because every time you talk to your clients (which is hopefully a lot), you're going to ask them how business is doing. If you've always had an interest in art and architecture, then focusing on architects and engineers might be a logical choice. If discussions of blood and body parts make you squeamish, you may not want to market to surgeons. If you think that this whole human genome thing is fascinating, then see how many genetics (and related) companies are nearby. You get the picture.

Part I
Set Meaningful Goals

CHAPTER 2

SETTING GOALS

For your business as an FA, setting goals is critical. I can go so far as to say that without proper goal setting, you'll flounder for a while and then fail. At best, you'll create the hardest and most unsatisfying low-paying job imaginable. Setting proper goals is the first step in creating a satisfying and lucrative career. Because goal setting is so important, that is our first step.

2.1 What Is a "Goal"?

A "goal" is simply a target. A desired result. You may have heard some variant of the following: A goal must be "SMART". That is, it must be *S*pecific, *M*easurable, *A*ttainable, *R*ealistic and *T*ime-targeted. Let's take those one at a time.

Specific

Specificity is key, and leads you to the other criteria. "Make a lot of money" is not specific enough. "A lot" never arrives because your definition of "a lot" continually changes. Put another way, your goalposts keep moving. However, if you change the wording to "make $450,000 per year in five years," that is specific enough.

Measurable

This is pretty straightforward. "Be happy" is not measurable. The 450k from our previous paragraph is. Paying off your student loans, or mortgage, or all debt–those are all measurable goals.

Attainable

Attainable and realistic overlap somewhat. In this context it means feasible or possible. Owning the moon is not attainable, no matter how hard you work.

Realistic

Realistic is a tough one. Have you heard the phrase "aim low and score"? An excessively low goal is easy to achieve, but unsatisfying to the point of being worthless. For example, "eat something other than peanut butter and jelly for lunch" is too achievable. It's no hurdle at all. At the other end of the spectrum, a goal of "make a $1,000,000 commission tomorrow" is probably unrealistic. An unrealistically high goal is one that is certain to fail, and can destroy your motivation to the point that you won't push yourself to achieve any goal. You should aim high enough that the goal has meaning and, when achieved, gives you satisfaction, but not so high that it is impossible.

Time-targeted

This is a facet that many people forget, but without a deadline, what you call a goal is little more than a fantasy. I'm all for fantasies, but not in business. So let's revisit our $450k income goal. By when? Forty years from now? Or five years? Setting a specific deadline is how we'll measure our progress.

2.2 A Practical Method of Setting Goals

There are plenty of methods to help you set goals. Some methods are overly simplistic and I've seen others that almost require advanced mathematics degrees. Would you rather (a) spend countless hours analyzing and re-analyzing how much money you might want to

2.2. A PRACTICAL METHOD OF SETTING GOALS

make if you ever start earning a living or (b) actually make money? If your answer is (a), please close this book. If, however, your answer is (b), let's dig in.

To quickly set your business goals, we're going to use two methods. The first is one based on your personal goals because personal goals should always drive business goals. The second method is more mundane. It's based on survival at your firm. Then we'll use the two methods to generate a final number for your business plan.

Method 1: Personal Goals Determine Business Goals

Step one is to list your personal goals. When I work with people helping them set their goals, many start with something like "I just want to be able to afford to pay all my bills on time, have some money left over to be able to enjoy life a little bit, oh and save money, too." But that sentence contains a number of goals and they all need to be *SMART*er. How much are your monthly bills? How much money left over? How much does it cost you to "enjoy life a little bit"? How much money do you want to save? And for each, when? That one vague statement could be expanded and turned into specific goals, as follows:

1. Pay all bills when due. Amount: $3,200 per month. What is the due-date for this goal? Now.
2. Pay off student loans ($14,000). I will pay them off in one lump sum exactly four years from today. To achieve this goal, I'll begin saving into a separate account on [date] and save according to the following schedule. [You create a schedule with specific amounts each month.] Savings will be invested in a money market fund.
3. Down payment on a house in XYX neighborhood. Approximate price range today: $250,000. Which equals a down payment of $50,000. I will have this money in the bank on [insert YOUR date here]. To achieve this goal, I'll begin saving

into a separate account on [date], and save according to the following schedule: [create schedule.] Savings will be invested in a money market fund.

4. Max out my 401(k) contributions each year, starting in two years. In [X] months, I'll begin contributing [4]% of my salary to the plan. In [Y] months I'll increase my savings to [8]%, and in [Z] months I'll increase my savings to the maximum. My account will be invested according to my financial plan and risk-tolerance profile.

5. To allow me to re-energize, I will take at least two weeks of vacation each year. Beginning on [DATE], I will save $X per month to fund my travel budget.

These are all simplistic and relatively short-term goals. For number one, you have to create a budget. How much does it cost you each month to live? For numbers two and three, figure out how much per month you need to save, on top of your living expenses, to have those two lump sums in the bank on the target dates that you set. For numbers four and five, figure the monthly amounts and add those to your budget each month. Although your list of goals will be different, the exercise is the same.

Now take those monthly numbers, which represent the amount of money you need to spend or save each month, and total them. A spreadsheet is highly recommended here. Factor in taxes and other deductions to get your monthly gross income targets. Now, what percentage of commissions do you receive? If you receive a different percentage of revenue based on the business line (e.g., individual stock trades versus managed money), you can probably talk with your supervisor to figure out a ballpark percentage. Whatever that number is, divide your income target by that percentage to determine your monthly and yearly fee/commission goals.

Method 2: The "Survival Method"

Let's not get fired, okay? If you're in your firm's training program, you probably received quarter-based revenue requirements ("hurdles"). Meeting those hurdles will help keep you from being fired for non-performance. Put those numbers into your spreadsheet.

Now take the monthly numbers you created in each method and for each quarter, choose the higher of the two numbers. Those are your goals. Once achieved, they will not only help you stay employed, but also will help you achieve your personal goals and build a good life for yourself.

2.3 Income Goals Determine Daily Activity

It's all well and good to say, "Yep, I've got a plan. I'm gonna rake in $137,000 of recurring revenue next year. Look, it's all charted out in my plan. It's awesome, right?" It actually is pretty cool. Congratulations. Before moving to the next step, let's review what we've done so far.

We've set goals. They are specific, measurable, attainable, reasonable, and time-targeted. (Note: we'll re-evaluate the attainability and reasonableness in the next step.) But what do you have to do to each and every day to achieve them? Action bridges the gap between idea and reality. Consistent daily action. We need to figure out the specific actions needed to acquire enough assets under management to hit those income targets.

It comes down to arithmetic again, so open a new page in your spreadsheet. Format it however you want, but don't spend a lot of time making it pretty. This is a tool, not a work of art. Use formulas in the spreadsheet so that when we tinker with the assumptions (making them more accurate), it will be fast and easy. You also need to pick a prospecting method, and we'll discuss those more later. For now we'll discuss cold calling as the prospecting example.

2.4 Setting the Numbers–Cold Calling

You need six numbers:
1. How many hours per week can you call?
2. How many cold calls ("dials") can you make in one hour?
3. From a block of 100 dials, how many "contacts" can you make? You're looking for a percentage.
4. From those contacts, how many appointments can you set?
5. From those appointments, how many accounts can you take over?
6. For your new accounts (heck yeah!), what is the average (or minimum) new account size? This translates into how much revenue you'll receive from the account.

Let's discuss each of those factors in a bit more detail. It will also help you to talk these through with your sales manager. He or she will know what other FAs are doing, the good ones and the bad. And here's a hint: You want to emulate the good FAs' work habits and ignore all others.

Calling Hours per Week

How many hours can you realistically call each week? Figure out how many work hours there are in a week. If you're calling individuals at their homes, the Do-Not-Call restrictions set the maximum hours. Even so, you won't be physically able to call every single minute that the FTC allows. Set up a model weekly work schedule and block out tasks. There are three types of tasks for an FA: (i) client acquisition; (ii) client service; and (iii) everything else. Just starting out, you have no clients to service so you should have no time spent on client service. The "everything else" includes research (which should be done in the evenings or on the weekends), internal meetings, etc.

2.4. SETTING THE NUMBERS–COLD CALLING

Maybe you decide that you'll make cold calls between nine o'clock and noon, then take a break for lunch, and call again from two to five in the afternoon. Six hours of calling per day equals thirty hours per week of calling, plus ten hours for lunch meetings with prospects. Note that if you calls at 9:00a.m., then you have time for breakfast meetings with prospects. Prospecting time is sacrosanct!

Cold Calls per Hour

Hopefully you've received training on cold calling and have scripted your call and the common objections. I think that your sales manager would be ecstatic if you came to him or her and asked for help with scripting. Think through the process of making the phone call: pick up and dial; the phone rings; you make your pitch to the suspect. You hang up and either make notes about the conversation, or you delete the contact from your list. If a gatekeeper answers instead, you have to pitch the gatekeeper before talking with the suspect. That adds time. If you get a hangup immediately, that makes the call shorter. If you get voice mail, do you leave one? That's your decision, but if you choose to leave a voice mail, make sure that you script it out exactly, and practice saying into the phone until it sounds natural and you're pleased with the way it sounds. Practice it on other people, leaving the message into their voice mailboxes. You need the constructive feedback. Over time, as you get better at calling, and as your targets get to know you, you will talk more and your calls per hour will decrease. That's fine because your success rates will correspondingly increase. All that being said, your number might be between 100 and 120 per hour.

Percentage of Calls That Become "Contacts"

First, what is a legitimate "contact"? When I was calling every day, I defined a contact as "a substantive discussion with a decision maker." You have to make your pitch to the person who has the power to make the decision to sign paperwork opening an account with you and transfer assets to your firm. Hangups don't count even if it is the decision maker who hangs up on you. If you're talking with the gatekeeper, a substantive discussion of the markets and the advantages of your firm may be valuable because it lays some groundwork for your next call, but it doesn't count as a contact. Over time, your actual experience will give you a fairly accurate contacts/calls ratio. For now, though, just insert a relatively low number, perhaps five or ten percent.

Percentage of Contacts That Set an Appointment

When you talk with the decision maker, your sole job is to qualify them and set an appointment. You only want to spend time with prospects you've pre-qualified. This number will also increase in proportion to your increasing skills. For now, set the ratio to around 10% and update it as you log actual data.

Percentage of Appointments That Open Accounts

At the appointment, your only goal is to "close the sale," which depends on factors including: (i) is the prospect truly "qualified"; (ii) is the prospect ready to make the move; (iii) do you and the prospect "click"; and (iv) your sales skills. Items (i) and (ii) depend on how well you pre-qualify the prospect. Item (iii) is also part of the pre-qualification process but many FAs don't care–they take any client they can get and worry about the quality of the client later. If a person is a jackass on the phone every single time you talk with them, they'll probably be a jerk in person, and even worse when you work for them. Whether you take them as a client is up to you, but my advice is that you should be picky. Taking a jerk as a client is a complaint (against you) waiting to happen. Finally, item (iv) depends on your sales skills, so make every effort to continually improve your craft.

Account Size

You need to set a firm number for how small of an account you will take. A $5,000 account takes the same amount of work as a $50,000 account. This is a business decision that is worth a discussion with your sales manager. My advice is to start thinking like a producer from the beginning. At a 1% revenue rate, a %50,000 account will earn you only $500 per year. If you want to make a quarter million per year, you'd have to have 500 accounts. It would be very difficult to properly service 500 accounts, and you'd have no life. So set a higher minimum from the beginning.

Part of the reason that I wrote this book, and part of the reason you are reading it is to help you market the fatter accounts. From the beginning, set a minimum of $100,000. Be a player. Players only take big accounts. (By the way, 100k is not big. A million is big. But in the beginning you have to compromise between speed of asset acquisition (*i.e.*, surviving) and being inflexible. Suppose, however, you meet a prospect that only has $99,000 of assets for you to manage. Move on? Of course not. Set a hard minimum (say $50,000). When you prospect, you tell your prospects that your minimum is $100,000. If they seem like a perfect client, other than the lack of assets, *and* it is very clear that there is great potential there, you can take them as a client. Make it clear that you are making an exception for them and that they need to get their assets over your minimum within a year or you'll have to have a "new FA" manage their account.

Account Revenue Rate

How much do you get paid on your accounts. It depends on your business model. Do you use managed accounts? Do you do only transactional, commission-based stock and bond trades? Do you focus on insurance? Or a combination of the above? Your sales manager can give you fairly accurate numbers for each type of business and help you come up with a number for your spreadsheet.

Table 2.1: Prospecting–Revenue Calculation

Calling hours per week	40	For your first week, this number should be 40, but it will decrease over time.
Calls per hour	100	
Contact percentage	8%	Out of 100 calls, you'll talk with the decision maker 8 times.
Appointment percentage	5%	Out of 100 contacts, you'll set an appointment 5 times.
"Close" rate	25%	You'll close one out of four appointments.
Avg account size	$50,000	
Account revenue rate	1%	Assumes fee-based business. For each $50,000 account, you'll earn $500 per year in fees.
Dials per new account:	1,000	Using these assumptions, for every 1,000 dials, you will gain one new account.

You calculate your total revenue from your average account size, not the minimum. As a rule of thumb, an FA's average account size might be about 2.5 times that FA's minimum. If you want to be conservative, use the minimum number as your average, at least in the beginning.

Let's start by working backwards. Suppose that your first quarterly target is to gain $250,000 in AUM (assets under management). That's five $50,000 accounts within three months, or .42 accounts per week (roughly). Let's say zero accounts the first two weeks and one account every other week thereafter. To get that one account, you need to have four meetings with qualified prospects (based on your 25% "close ratio"). To set up four meetings, you need to have 80 "contacts" with decision makers. To get those 80 contacts, you'll need to make 1,000 cold calls. At 100 calls per hour, it will take 10

2.4. SETTING THE NUMBERS–COLD CALLING

hours to make 1,000 cold calls. That can be done in two or three days.

It sounds easy. The numbers in Rows 3 and 4 are high to start off with. I've had times where I've made two hundred dials and didn't get a single contact. Then I've gotten an appointment on the next two calls and on the next five calls the suspect asked for further contact (in other words, they said, "I am interested in talking with you, but not right now because of XYZ reason, so please call me back after such-and-such date.) So if you think that all you have to do is work a day and a half each week and you'll be a success, that's wrong! For your first week of calling, make it your goal to call as many suspects as you can, so you can start to get realistic numbers for the equation.

Over time, your ratios will become more accurate. (Note that every person's ratios are different, so don't compare yours to anyone else's.) Not after the first day or even the first week, though. Only time will tell what your ratios actually are, but once you figure them out, you know exactly how many hours you need to call in order to achieve your goals. More good news is that, for a few reasons, your hours calling will decrease over time. First, you'll improve your skills and your ratios will get better. Second, you'll talk to the same people enough times that they'll get to know you, and trust you, and you'll be more likely to win an appointment. Finally, as you build your client base, you'll need to spend less time on prospecting (which is good because you'll have less time for prospecting).

Again, your ratios will be different. For the first month, cold call a couple hundred calls a day and track your results. Replace the estimates in your spreadsheet with your actual ratios. Then you'll know that for your target audience and your skill level you'll have a decent approximation of how many hours per day you need to call.

The bad news is that I can pretty much guaranty to you that it will take more than a couple of hours of cold calls to get you one account. Especially at first. You've got to stick with it until the ratios work in your favor. Trust me, with work they will. Also, as you set appointments regularly, those appointments will cut into your prospecting time. Your calling time will decrease. Compensate for that. Make sure that you still make enough calls in the day. And finally, as you begin to build a client base, you now have to spend time serving those clients, which further takes away from your prospecting/calling time.

Now that you have a chart of calling ratios and numbers, put it into your business plan. This gives you the tangible connection between your goals and the daily action that will make it possible for you to achieve those goals. Also, putting it in writing helps you to be accountable. If your goal is 400 calls per day, what happens if you miss a day? Do you make up those calls over the next couple of days? (The answer is "YES WITHOUT FAIL BECAUSE I'M GOING TO SUCCEED DAMMIT!") But you get my point. Once the plan is in writing, you commit to it. Tell your significant other, your mom, your mastermind group, your therapist, or whomever. But commit to it publicly and incorporate it into your day.

Motivate Yourself

To keep you going, day in, day out, lifting the receiver, dialing, putting up with the same objections, *ad nauseum*, think about this. To gain one $50,000 account, you need to dial 1,000 times. At a 1% revenue rate, that account will pay $500 in fees per year. So, just for the first full year, that one dial is worth fifty cents to you. A day's worth of cold calls is worth a hundred bucks to you. If you can keep the account for ten years, each dial is worth five dollars. That's not including the account's growth. Think about that when you're dialing. "Here's five bucks." Dial. Talk. Hang up. "Here's five bucks." Dial. Talk. Set appointment. Hang up. "Here's five bucks." Dial. Talk. Hang up. One dial closer to the next appointment. And so on.

Cold calling is like driving the interstates through the midwest. Each mile is boring. (I mean no offense by this. I'm from the midwest, and I recognize boring.) But you keep focusing on the goal. A hundred miles, five hundred, on and on. You hit your goal. The numbers prove it.

2.5 Other Prospecting Methods

The previous exercise used cold calling as the example. Oddly enough, many people hate cold calling. So let's talk about other prospecting methods.

With every prospecting method, some people love it and some people hate it. The key is to find a method you like, systematize it, schedule it, and stick with your schedule. Once you figure out how much time each step of the process really takes, then you create a realistic schedule to allow the numbers to push enough people in front of you to win enough accounts to hit all your goals. The schedule helps you achieve the goals. For example, it doesn't make sense to address envelopes in the middle of the day. Instead, in the daytime you should be meeting with prospects, calling to follow up on invitations sent, etc. You address envelopes in the evening, or otherwise not in those prime or sacrosanct hours.

Seminars

What could be better? You invite a bunch of rich folk to dinner and talk about some hot topic (making money). The numbers still apply. The process for setting up and holding dinner seminars is more involved than cold calling, and requires more lead time: get a list, send out invitations, make follow up calls to the invitees, have the seminar, set follow up appointments, then go to the appointment and close the sale. In addition to the mechanics of invitations and follow-up phone calls, you have to plan an interesting seminar and practice your talk. And then do it all over again for the next seminar, because you need to have more than one seminar to be a success.

To get one account, you need to have Z follow-up appointments. To have Z follow-up appointments, you need to have Y people at your seminar. To have Y people at your seminar, you need to have X people confirm (there are always no-shows, so plan ahead). To have X people confirm, you need to invite W people. If seminars are your chosen method, you need to change the spreadsheet accordingly and then plan out a schedule. I know FAs who have seminars once per week and they've reduced the process to a science.

If you want to use seminars as your primary prospecting method, you will have some challenges. The first challenge is logistics. Suppose that you start with the assumption that you'll need to have one seminar every month to be able to hit your goals. You might set up the following schedule:

Day 1: Decide on a location. If you are funding the seminar yourself, it's your choice. If a wholesaler is funding it, talk with the wholesaler to get her or his advice. Confirm the date, time and location with the wholesaler (make sure it's on his or her calendar), confirm with the restaurant and make the reservation. Order invitations.

Day 7: Invitations arrive. Begin addressing envelopes. I think that hand writing addresses would not be feasible. Mailing labels are significantly faster, but have a more "salesy" look. The fastest way would be to run the envelopes directly through the laser printer. So you need your mailing list in a database that will handle envelopes, the printer has to be able to handle that size of envelope, and it would be nice if you can use a decent typeface. After the envelopes are addressed, you have to stuff them.

Day 9: Mail the envelopes.

Day 12-14: Begin calling recipients to follow up on the invitations. Confirm they received it (they did), ask if they are interested, etc., and *sell* them on the seminar. The length of time the calls will take depends on how many you call and how many calls you can make per day. It should be faster than a cold call, so you might be able to do 300 per day without too much trouble. For this illustration, let's say you complete the calls in five

2.5. OTHER PROSPECTING METHODS 19

days.

Day 15-20: Meet with your wholesaler/sponsor. Work out an outline of the evening. Then "script" your talk. Whatever process you use to make speeches–whatever process is best for you–use it now. You have to make the talk interesting. So begin to practice now so that at the seminar you sound natural and engaging.

Day 27-29: Call each attendee to confirm. If applicable, make sure compliance has approved all handouts, etc., and you've assembled professional-looking packets for each invitee.

Day 30: Seminar. Thank each attendee personally and get commitment to meet with you to discuss how the seminar topic specifically affects them.

Day 31: Call to follow up with each attendee. Set appointments.

As you can see from the model timeline, if you wanted to do two seminars per month, you would have two of these cycles running concurrently. Or, hold the same seminar on two or three nights and invite more people so that you can fill three nights of seminars.

The second challenge is funding. Seminars cost money and it's harder to get people to pay for them than it used to be. But you have to ask. I'd ask your sales manager to start with, because your SM will know the funding "climate," which wholesalers to approach, and how to get you started.

There are a lot of good resources on seminars and I would bet that many of them are only paces away from your desk. If there is an FA or team in your office who does a lot of seminars, ask them for tips. Ask if you could "shadow" them or help them out in return for learning how to do a good job on seminars. (You'll want to reassure them that you're not going to try to poach their clients or prospects.) Ask your wholesalers about topics, methods and best practices. They see more seminars than anyone else. There are even some books, of course, for your weekend reading pleasure.

Networking

Networking is great. Your "ratios" will quickly rise to amazing (when compared to cold calling) levels because your prospects can get to know you much more quickly than through a series of cold calls. But the most common "rookie" mistake that I've seen is that they turn "networking" into "not working," which kills careers. For a networking event to qualify, you have to have meaningful contact with a person you suspect may have the potential to be a qualified prospect, and you have to have some agreement to have further contact. Get their card with the closing phrase, "Hey, let's go to breakfast next week. I'd love to hear more about your business. Can I call you this afternoon to set a time?" Or something like that. I'd suggest that you don't say, "Hey, I'd love to tell you more about my business." Client service is all about them, not about how great you are or how smart your firm's "really smart people in New York" are.

There are plenty of books on how to network and where to network. I've listed a few in the appendices. I read them and they were useful and worth the price.

Notes on "Mining your Client List"

When I was in my training program, all the time wholesalers would show us wonderful ways to "mine" our client lists. Meaning how to cross sell and up sell to existing clients. That's great for an established producer but frankly, it's worthless for rookies. You don't really have a "minable" client list until you're established.

For these lunch meetings, enjoy the lunch, smile and take notes, then put those notes into a special file. Maybe the file is called "tactics for the future." Or maybe the file would be more . . . circular in form.

Instead, talk to the wholesaler after the lunch, one on one. Say something like, "That was great information and your product sounds fantastic. But I have zero clients. Could I pick your brain about ways to market your product to new folks?" They'll be more than

2.5. OTHER PROSPECTING METHODS

happy to help you and they'll likely tell you what's working for other producers. Especially if you ask them, "What's working for other FAs?"

CHAPTER 3

CONFIDENCE AND ATTITUDE

YOU must have confidence in order to be any good at sales. Every human has the angel on one shoulder and a demon on the other. Starting off, the demon beats you down with whispers of, "You're so new, what do you know about this," or "What makes you better than their current advisor?" If that's the thought that sticks in your brain all day long, you're done. You need to give the angel the ammunition to fire back, so you can keep the motivation to pick up the phone again and again.

Self confidence and motivation is like a shower: It must be reinforced daily. Pick a couple of books that focus on confidence, read them in your spare time and highlight the passages that resonate with you. Buy some audio programs on confidence and motivation and listen to them on the way to work or on the way to an appointment. It helps.

One of the big issues that will plague you is that of the naysayer. Every group has one. Or two.... When I was in my training program, the office's biggest naysayers was one of our training "coaches." Ironic, right? At one of my periodic meetings with him, he asked me how I planned on prospecting. I told him networking. He sucked in his breath, sat back in his chair and and began to pontificate to me. "Well, it seems like every couple of days I get a young trainee in here saying that they want to build their business by networking. And I'll tell you that in all the years that I've been doing this, I've never seen a single one of them succeed. I've never seen an advisor succeed by relying on netwoking." I responded, "I don't believe in fighting the numbers, so tell me, in all of your years of experience, what way has the highest probability of success?" Obviousaly self-satisfied, he puffed himself up and told me all of the virtues of cold calling.

At my next meeting with him, he asked me the same question. So this time I answered "cold calling," and listed some of the positives that he had recited to me a few weeks earlier. The funny thing was that then he gave me the exact same speech! "I've never seen an advisor succeed by relying on cold calling." It was almost verbatim. That was when I realized that he was a "coach" not to help people but to help himself feel superior. He was (and probably still is) a naysayer. Whatever you're doing, he'll tell you that it's wrong. If you have sound reasons behind your decision, he'll find some other way to put you down. My best advice for getting past these people? Remember that they're small people and they are afraid of you surpassing them. Just keep your head down, ignore them, laugh it off when they walk away, and then surpass them. Then go and tell them how wrong they were.

These people are toxic. Avoid them.

Part II

Choosing a Niche

CHAPTER 4

NOTES ON "NATURAL MARKETS"

STARTING out in this business, you'll hear a lot of people tell you to your "natural market." I'll make it plain and simple. Most rookies should ignore their natural market, at least for a while. A "natural market" is a group of people a lot like you. Similar age, background, income level, net worth, and interests. So if you're a debt-laden broke 25 year old who plays video games in all spare time, I'd suggest that you may not want to spend a lot of time prospecting people like you. (I don't mean that as an insult. When I graduated from college, I was debt laden myself. I wouldn't have prospected me!)

If, however, you spend your weekends at your family's country club or yacht club (or would like to) and you're on a first-name basis with the "one percenters" out there, there may be a valid reason to focus some effort on your natural market. If you do, however, decide to focus some time on this market, take a strategic and more subtle approach. They know you as a "kid." Sorry, but all "old rich people" look at anyone under 40 or 50 as a "kid." They look at you as that cute kid who one day wanted to be a fireman, the next week an astronaut, then a nuclear engineer, then a doctor, etc., but now you're telling them that they can trust you with their money. Their money that they accumulated by suffering through decades of 80-hour weeks. Their life savings that they protected through four recessions, twelve substantial market crashes, two divorces, and so on. A standard up-front pitch of "I'd like to sit down with you and show you how we're different and how we can make your financial situation better" will likely fall on deaf ears. (No pun intended.)

Work into it slowly. Don't try to sell them initially. You've got to build your credibility. If they ask how your job is going: "I'm learning a lot. I'm working with a team (or a senior advisor) and learning great techniques to maintain returns but protect your principal, reduce risk, etc." Slowly build that up until you're the one with the knowledge. In a bull market, they'll ask for for a tip. They always do. Their question is partly a test, so you have to have an answer. But part of it is that they just want a free tip. Never give them a specific tip. When they ask for a tip, tell them that it depends on their portfolio and their specifics and that you normally do an in-depth analysis before making any specific recommendation. But then add, "While the bull market makes it seem like an investor can't lose, the market/economy has a lot of risk built in, so you have to be careful. Just as important as making money is not losing money, don't you think?" Your statement is always true, and their answer is always yes. Then you say, "If that sounds worthwhile to explore, I'd be happy to get my team together and review your current strategy." First, that sounds a lot better than asking them for time so you can show them how you can do better. And second, even if they don't nibble on that bait, it will stay in their minds. After the bull market comes the bear market. Then your friends will bitch and moan about how they "lost" XXX thousand dollars. More accurately, how their "brokers" lost that money for them. Now you step in and tell them that's why your team spends so much time during the bull markets implementing your strategies. It's to protect your clients during the inevitable downturns. So, Ms. Friend, would you like to do something about this to make your hard-earned money more secure, before the next bear market hits?

CHAPTER 5

BUSINESS OWNERS AS A NICHE

BUSINESS owners can be awesome clients. They really can. When I was an FA, I found that the owners of established small businesses were great to work with. Here are some of the reasons:

1. They're hard working. This means that they like hard-working people, so you have to convey to them that you'll work hard for their interests once you have their accounts.
2. They're very goal-oriented, which is good for creating and implementing a financial plan.
3. They're decisive. They makes decisions quickly.

In addition, small-business clients can be very lucrative for your practice:

1. The owner of a successful business generally has a significant income and net worth.
2. Many cross sell opportunities.
3. Their accounts tend to grow over time as they make and invest more and look for more ways to invest and protect their hard-earned money.

5.1 The Demographics of Business Owners

Read "The Millionaire Next Door" by Thomas Stanley. That will tell you all about business owners and their mindsets. Next, read the other Stanley books that I recommend in the "Resources" chapter.

Generally, there is a direct positive correlation between successful business owners and personal wealth. Looking at high net worth individuals, as net worth increases (e.g., $1-10 million, $10-25 million, and so on), the higher the percentage of of business owners.

Business owners are decisive. They have a quick, decision-making mindset. I found that once you present them with the facts, they will make a decision very quickly whether they want to know more or whether you absolutely cannot help them. If they want to know more, you're halfway to the sale. They won't waste their time by wasting your time.

The flip side is that you have to have your presentation down cold. Focus on demonstrable and provable facts. No sales BS. If you can, have case studies. "Ms. Owner, this is how we helped one of your competitors." (Note: Take out all identifying data.) The main point is that you won't get a lot of responses like, "I'll think about it. Can you call me back in a few weeks?"

You'll find a variety of industries, which gives you the opportunity to focus on specific businesses. Law firm partners are the owners of the law firm. Same with anyone else called "partner." Medical practices, accounting firms, architectural firms, home improvement companies, etc. You have plenty of opportunity to choose a "specialty." And business owners prefer specialists (i.e., experts) over generalists (i.e., a jack of all trades).

5.2 Business Owners' Needs

Business owners have a diverse array of needs. Hopefully, your firm has products and services targeted toward each of these needs. For example, each of the following potential needs, may be solved by solutions your firm might offer.

Finding and retaining top-quality employees
> → Employee benefits (state-of-the-art retirement / profit-sharing plans)

Cash management

→ Better types of cash management accounts (lower fees, higher yields)
→ Increasing yield on excess cash balances.
→ Credit card solutions

Investment opportunities
→ Wide range of robust investments

Estate planning needs
→ Life insurance
→ Trust planning
→ Wealth transfer strategies

Funding buyout arrangements in "shareholder" agreements
→ Life insurance alternatives

Tax planning
→ Tax-efficient investments and investment strategies

Growth strategies
→ Investment banking
→ Financing
→ Financial planning

Exit strategies
→ Investment banking
→ Wealth transfer strategies
→ Retirement income planning

Hedging
→ Diversification
→ Financial planning
→ Alternative investments

Extremely high profits
→ Executive comp plan
→ The so-called "super Roth"
→ Tiered retirement plan structure: 401(k) + profit-sharing formulas beneficial to the owner + defined benefit plan
→ Captive insurance companies to shelter "excess" profits in a potentially triple tax free structure

Create scripts and talking points each applicable need and how you and your firm provide a solution. For example:

FA: "Ms. Owner, are you satisfied with the yield your current bank gives you?"

Owner: "Are you kidding? Zero percent? No, I'm not happy, but how can you earn more?"

FA: "My firm has conservative programs available where you can earn between X and Y percent. You mentioned that you normally keep about [two million] dollars in your corporate bank account. If we re-allocated just half of that balance, you could earn an additional [$XX,000] per year. Would it be worth an hour of your time to discuss this in more detail? I'll do an analysis and then we can see if one of our strategies is right for you."

Owner: "Well, I don't know. I'm really busy."

FA: "I understand. Let's play this out, though. The worst case scenario is that we find out that it's not right for you and then you know that you're doing the best you can. The best-case, however, is that for that one hour, and the couple of additional hours it will take to set things up, you increase your revenue by [$XX,000]. That's a pretty good hourly rate, don't you think?"

Owner: "Yes, it is. Can you meet with me at 7:00 in the morning? That way nobody will interrupt us."

FA: "Absolutely. I meet a lot of my business-owner clients early in the day. How's you're schedule? What day are you looking at?" [Note: Don't accept the first date that he/she offers. Don't look desperate. You're a busy FA, even if you just started your business. Create the appearance!]

5.3 Finding Business Owners

There are two ways to get a list: (i) buying a list; and (ii) building a list (data mining). Buying a list, of course, costs money. The better the list, the more it costs you—either in time or in effort. My advice: Do both.

Trust me on this. I'm good at creating lists and I've done it for a lot of FAs. I've created lists for newbies as well as extremely successful FAs. They've all told me that I created a damn good list for them. Build a good list, then call the livin' hell out of it. Then, you will succeed.

The first question you have to answer is how big of a list you need. You need enough "suspects" to allow you to try to contact them once per month while keeping you calling for the entire month.

How Many Prospects?

Now that you've decided to focus on a particular segment of business owners, you need to generate a list of contacts. More specifically, a list of suspects that you will turn into prospects and then clients. How many names do you need? If you make 200 cold calls per day, that's 1,000 per week and 4,000 per month (roughly). So you need a list of 4,000 somewhat-qualified suspects (remember, you'll turn these suspects into prospects).

Let's go back to our first spreadsheet where we figured out how many calls you'll need to make to hit your revenue goals. In that exercise, we determined that you need to call 1,000 suspects per week. If you're going to try to talk with each contact once per month, you'll need "about" 4,000 contacts in your prospecting list.

You'll want to get more names than the numbers actually require. The first time that you talk to a person, it may become obvious that either they will never do business with you (for whatever reason) or you would never want to do business with them. If your list is too small, you'll quickly run out of names to call. Build in a factor of safety to account for the fact that your list may decrease in size by a significant number in the first couple of months. And don't worry about immediately deleting a contact from your spreadsheet. I've had people tell me, "I appreciate your call, but there's no chance...."

Maybe a relative is their current FA. Maybe they do it themselves. Whatever the reason, don't waste your time by trying to change the unchangeable.

If we set a goal of making 4,000 calls per month, you'll probably want a list of 5,000 contacts.

Not Enough Widget Manufacturers?

That's a valid concern. The solution is simple. Target two or three markets. For example, if you choose architects, you might also want to choose construction companies, contractors, and subcontractors. Lawyers and accountants are also complimentary. If you choose lawyers and CPAs, for your third market add an unrelated (but still lucrative) market (we'll use plumbers as an example). You develop the lawyer/CPA markets as clients and then as referral sources. At some point, one of your third market plumber clients will ask for a referral to a lawyer or an accountant. You refer them to one of your lawyer or CPA clients, as appropriate. That also sets up a mutual referral relationship, which will be beneficial to you over the long term.

Buying a List

Buying a list is easy. Yes, it will cost you a few bucks, but you've got to spend money to make money, right? It's an investment in your future and will save you time. When you consider whether to buy a list or scrape data from multiple sources to build a list, you have to answer four questions:

(i) Do you have enough money in the bank or under the bed so that you could buy the list without putting your existing bills in jeopardy?

(ii) If you don't have the cash to buy the list, could you responsibly borrow it? This means that if you "put it on a card" you have to have a plan to pay it back. From a planning standpoint, would you recommend to one of your clients to borrow money at high interest rates to invest in some speculative venture? Physician, heal thyself (meaning, take your own advice).

(iii) How much is your time worth today? If your base salary is $50,000, your hour is worth twenty-five dollars. You should never do anything that's worth less than $25 per hour. If someone will do your laundry for five dollars an hour, and it takes you four hours to do laundry, you should pay them to do your laundry and prospect for those hours.

(iv) Similarly, how much do you want to make a year from now? If you want to make a hundred thousand per year (which equates to $50 per hour), you should do nothing that is worth less than that amount. Re-read item (iii) above.

There are three sources that I'd currently recommend you consider: Larkspur and/or Judy Diamond Associates ("JDA"), and Dun & Bradstreet ("D&B"). Each source has advantages and disadvantages, but all will get you where you need to go. You want to target profitable businesses. You can either buy a list from D&B with your specific sales and profitability criteria, or you can "back door" your way into the information by using Larkspur or JDA.

Larkspur and JDA

Theoretically, if a company has no profits, it cannot fund a profit-sharing plan. Take this another step and you can say that a company with a nice fat qualified profit-sharing plan is *probably* flush with cash. That's the "back door." You can use that information to obtain a list from either JDA or Larkspur. One word of caution: I mentioned retirement plans. I would suggest that you *don't* focus primarily on gaining the qualified plan business. There is too much lead time between first contact and closing the sale. Focus on the services that you can offer the business today, as well as the business owner's personal investments. In a few years ask for the plan assets. Here's an exception to that rule, though. If the plan seems like it's low hanging fruit, then grab it. For example, if you're looking at the owner's account in his company's 401(k) plan, and you see that he's paying too much in sales charges for the mutual funds, then definitely bring that up. "Hey, Ms. Owner, do you know that you're paying twice as much for these mutual funds as you should be? I'm sure your existing broker enjoys the extra income, but if you don't like paying $X,000 per year unnecessarily, I could fix that for you. Do you want me to take a look?"

Where does this data come from? If a company has a qualified retirement plan, such as a 401(k), at the end of each year, the company prepares and files a form to maintain its "qualification" under IRS regulations. After filing, certain information is made public. Companies such as JDA and Larkspur compile and organize the data, then make it available to subscribers.

Once you get access to the database (either JDA or Larkspur), you begin to pre-qualify the leads so that you are not calling companies that are not worth your time. Search for:

1. The company is located near you.
2. The plan has a balance between 1,000,000 and five to ten million dollars. Tiny plans are (in most cases) not worth your time and large plans have extremely long sales cycles.
3. The plan has an average participant balance over $40,000.
4. The company is privately-owned.
5. The plan is not part of a collective bargaining agreement.
6. You can also filter by SIC or NAICS codes to return only one industry but that may generate too few results.

Store that data in a spreadsheet for actual calling purposes.

Larkspur

Some retirement plan wholesalers have provided Larkspur passwords to FAs who wish to prospect businesses. Ask them. Whether they

5.3. FINDING BUSINESS OWNERS

can help you, in my experience, doesn't depend on your production or how much business you have done with the particular wholesaler. It depends on whether the wholesaler's company has set up the relationship with Larkspur. Even if you're just going into production, the wholesaler will be happy to help you because they know that when you prospect for retirement plan business, they'll get the chance to bid for business. Don't hesitate to ask the wholesaler; get them on your team.

JDA

Judy Diamond Associates competes with Larkspur. To buy the list of all plans in Arizona, JDA charges $900 for all 12,000 leads. That includes the public information on the plan and the company.

Suppose you live or work in Washington, DC. You'd want to be able to prospect not only the District, but also Virginia and Maryland–the entire DC metropolitan area. Where, buying the data for all three "states" (for trivia purposes, of those three jurisdictions, Maryland is the only state: DC is not a state, and Virginia is one of our nation's four commonwealths) would cost $2,700 (for about 40,000 leads), you could buy the entire Southern Mid Atlantic database (which includes the District of Columbia, Maryland, Virginia and West Virginia) for $1,700. Sure, you're buying West Virginia, but buying the regional database is cheaper than buying only the three states you need.

Although at some point you will ask for retirement plan business, to start off you prospect the company's general business and the business owner's personal business. Once you get that account, you'll begin to market your client to take over new pieces of business, including the retirement plan. I apologize for being repetitive, but I've seen many budding careers killed by FAs who went solely for retirement plan business. Again, the lead time is too long.

Cleaning the Larkspur (and JDA) Data

The information has two problems, though. First, the Larkspur and JDA data is always a year or so out of date. It's not their fault; it's just because of the way the government releases the data. Don't get hung up on that fact though. You primarily want the company names, addresses and phone numbers.

Second, the contact name identified has always been the person who prepared the plan's tax return. It might be the CFO, the Human Resources Manager, the President/CEO, or the owner. In many cases, though, it's the "office manager." On occasion, it's the name of a third party that does nothing but prepare the form. When you're prospecting, you still want to ask for the owner so you'll need to do a little legwork to figure out who is the person you need to talk to (*i.e.*, the owner or the President/CEO).

So how do you get the owner's name? Well, you could call the company and say, "Hi, this is Joe from XYZ Financial, could you connect me to the owner?" The receptionist knows that you're cold calling and most likely hang up on you. Or, you could be modestly clever and call the receptionist and say something like:

> Note: With this whole conversation, you need to play "Columbo" on the receptionist. You're the pitiful, downtrodden lackey, with an overbearing boss making you do all of the grunt work. The receptionist identifies with this. Don't let her think that your the wily wizard of Wall Street that you actually are.

> **FA:** "Hi, this is Joe from XYZ Financial. My boss told me to send your company's president some information, but my boss's handwriting is terrible. (Laugh a little bit.) He has a bunch of names here but no titles next to the names. Is [NAME FROM DATABASE] the company's owner or President? My boss told me to get it in the mail today and he's in a meeting. I've tried everything and then I realized that maybe I could just call. (Sound somewhat exasperated!)

5.3. FINDING BUSINESS OWNERS

Is there any way you can help me?" Hopefully, the receptionist will try to be helpful and not pass you through to them, because in most cases it won't be the owner. The receptionist will say,

Receptionist: "No, he's the CFO."

FA: "Oh, thanks. I think that makes sense. He wants a copy to each of them. Could you help me out with the owner's name?"

After the receptionist gives you the name, verify the spelling of the names, and the company's name and address. Seriously, verify the spelling, and use a phonetic spelling if necessary to differentiate between an "F" and an "S". I once knew a senior FA who had a newbie call companies on his behalf. The kid made a whole day's worth of phone calls, but didn't properly verify the information. On the first contact, the kid got the name wrong because of an "F" versus "S" pronunciation, then he got the email wrong, and it took two phone calls from the kid and one email bounced back to the senior FA (the kid got the email address wrong, too) before the senior FA just deleted that contact and the rest of the kid's work. After that demonstration of incompetence, what are the chances of that contact becoming a prospect, let alone a client? Yeah, zero. The senior FA also threw away all of the other contacts the kid made.

You don't have to ham it up that much, but get into the mood and make the receptionist feel sorry for you. Now, you may wonder whether it might be a little dishonest to call them and say something that is not strictly accurate. But think about it. When you tell your sales manager that you are going to target small and mid-sized business, he/she will tell you to contact the owner and begin prospecting, which includes sending them some information. So while your boss didn't mention that company specifically, he/she probably pointed to your list and said that about all companies in the list. So your statement is absolutely true.

The advantage of calling first to get the owner's name is that when you cold call them for real, you'll ask for an actual person rather than asking blindly for "the owner," which is as bad as sending a letter to "occupant." The only downside is that it will take some time. Many people will disagree with the strategy, but in my experience it works. Regarding how to deal with naysayers, please see my note in the short chapter on confidence.

There is a downside, though. While you call and identify of the owner, President/CEO, or CFO, you're not marketing. You could bring in an intern to make those non-marketing phone calls for you. And perhaps you could talk with your compliance officer to see if you could make those calls before you're licensed. After all, if an intern could make the calls on behalf of an FA, shouldn't you be allowed to make the same phone calls as long as your script was approved? If not, you could devote the first two weeks of production making "who's the owner" calls. For each day, try to make double the actual number of cold calls as in your business plan. That will let you work your list as quickly as possible so you can start calling (and selling) for real. Once you start selling, try to make up the missed calls over the first month.

Bottom line? Yes, it will take a little work, but you now have a list that didn't cost anything out of pocket.

Dun & Bradstreet Lists

In my opinion, the best general business lists come from Dun & Bradstreet. They always have. D&B lists offer you high quality information, but they are relatively expensive. To get individual contact information, D&B charges between $1.20 and $1.50 per lead as of January 2014. That price includes the company name, address, your target's name, and the direct phone number. After D&B bought Hoover's, D&B's retail list portal is located at *www.hoovers.com*.

If you wanted to try to be economical, you could reduce the cost to $0.36 per lead by buying only the company's name, address and

Table 5.1: Comparison of List Sources

Source	Advantages	Disadvantages
JDA	convenient	costs money; requires data cleaning; can't search for annual sales or profits
Larkspur	convenient; free access probably available	requires data cleaning; can't search for annual sales or profits
D&B	high-quality, current data; will provide direct phone number to top officer; list is ready to call	costs money

main phone number. That would cost only $2,700 for 7,500 contacts. But then for each company you'd have to call and find out the owner's name.

Also, ask your wholesalers (all of them, not just the retirement plan wholesalers) and ask if they can help you out with a list of business owners. Either just giving you one that matches your criteria, or whether they can get a discount with D&B or JDA. Remember that the two big differences between D&B and JDA/Larkspur is that (i) D&B offers accurate data for the owner, CEO, CFO and other key employees, but they charge you for it, and (ii) JDA and Larkspur may be cheaper or even free, but you'll need to work around the fact that they don't have contact information for the owner. Everything in life involves trades and compromises.

5.4 Data Mining

With the internet, data mining is easy, but it is still somewhat time consuming. First locate the industry's trade or professional association. Check its website. If you're lucky, it will let you search for members. If you don't know if there's an industry or trade association, search the internet until you find it (or them).

For example, if I search for "architects trade association" I get hits that include the American Institute of Architects (the "AIA"), which is the primary professional association for architects, as well as the "Architectural Contractors Trade Association of Michigan." The latter may be useful for a Michigan-based practice, but otherwise probably not.

Your local convention center is another good source for business leads and other niche leads. Bookmark your convention center's website. If you are targeting the construction industry, look for related shows. The "home show" or "home improvement" show, would probably have contractors exhibiting. The spring boat show would have boat dealers, custom boat builders, maritime insurance agents, finance companies, waterfront communities, etc. All of those are businesses. And who buys boats? People with money.

At one boat show I attended, I walked past a boat finance company and I semi-eavesdropped on the salesman's pitch. As soon as he gave the rate and down-payment requirement, I said under my breath (but I wanted the guy next to me to hear), "That's not a good deal. My company could finance the same boat for half the interest rate and we'd finance the whole thing." The guy standing next to me immediately turned to me and asked for more information. I turned him into a client. I don't want you to torpedo someone else's sales pitch, but there's nothing wrong with catching someone as they either walk up to or walk away from a display booth. So watch the convention center's web site and put interesting shows on your calendar. They are great places to prospect.

Are you targeting medical practices? There's an extremely quick, easy and no-cost way to build a high-quality list. In my forthcoming book on marketing to medical professionals, I detail the method step-by-step.

Businesses will be profiled in your city's local business journal, such as Crain's Chicago Business, Crain's New York Business, or the Baltimore Business Journal (just to give three examples). The local business journal publishes an annual Book of Lists. Crain's New York Business, for example, includes list of the top privately-owned businesses, the top law firms and accounting firms (according to the number of professionals), women-owned businesses, minority-owned businesses, fastest-growing companies, architectural firms, engineering firms, and more. Buy it on disk and you can copy and paste these highly-successful businesses into your call list. You should read your local business journal throughout the year. Your prospects do. Look at the ads. The advertisers might be potential prospects. Look at the articles about local businesses. Businesses make the news because they're doing good things, including making money. Opening a new plant or hiring new people? Maybe now's the time to talk with the owner about the benefit package (e.g., the profit-sharing plan). Add these to your list and contact them every month. Call them and congratulate them on making the paper. Have the article framed, mail it to the CEO, and then call him a few days later. It's that simple. Although it won't give you an instant list of four to five thousand names that you can start calling on day one, it will let you add good suspects to your list every month.

5.5 Prospecting Business Owners

We prospect business owners in many different ways. Whatever prospecting method you enjoy, you can probably use it to meet business owners.

In any event, there are ways to enhance your expertise and credibility within the industry. For your chosen industry, search the internet for applicable professional or trade associations. Join them and subscribe to any industry journals. Many associations have membership categories for vendors. This creates opportunities network at national and regional meetings, gives you the chance to sponsor or offer educational programs (maybe a seminar or webinar on "Six Ways To Increase your Cash Flow," for example), and increases your credibility within the industry.

Reading the trade journals will give you valuable information: Who are the industry "players," current issues, etc. It also gives you something to talk about. For example, when you talk to a prospect, you can ask, "Did you see the XYZ Association article on [topic]? It's generating a lot of discussion right now. What are your thoughts on that issue?" If they agree that it's an issue, you can add, "At my company, we researched the issue and have some unique solutions. Would that be something you'd like to hear about?" If they are interested, ask to sit down for a half hour or so.

Take this next point with a grain of salt, because I'm not really a "dinner seminar" guy. That being said, I've found that business owners are not all that receptive to lunch seminars or dinner seminars. I found that it's easier to ask them for a personal meeting. One tactic that did work for me was to call the business owners to invite them to a lunch seminar. If they decline because of time, say something like, "I understand. Hmmm, you know what? I bet that I could save you some time by coming to your office, and without all of the questions and so forth that we'd get in the group environment without the 'overhead.' We could do that in about a half hour." If you've talked with the person for a few minutes, you might be able to add something like, "I can't offer this to everyone, but I've enjoyed our talk."

Qualifying Business Owners

When you're building a list, you need to pre-screen or pre-qualify the potential leads. Then as you talk to them, you fully qualify them.

5.5. PROSPECTING BUSINESS OWNERS

You've been trained to qualify prospects, so let's focus on the first step, which is getting a good list.

Within your chosen industry, focus on businesses that satisfy the following criteria:

1. Privately owned.
2. Annual sales between $5,000,000 and $100,000,000. You'll want to play with the searches to narrow your range. How many local businesses are there with sales between $10 million and $50 million? If there are too many, narrow the criteria. Not enough? Reduce the lower end of the range and recalculate. Watch the upper end of the sales range, though. Too big means too much effort, too much red tape, and too much time to close a sale. Leave it to someone else.
3. Profitable for at least three of the last five years.
4. Willingness and ability to do business with you.
5. The decision maker grants you permission to call back.

The first three items can be used as search terms in the D&B database. The fourth item should be discussed in either your first or second conversation with the contact. The fifth item would be discussed in the first phone call. Only if the contact satisfies all of these criteria can you legitimately call them a "prospect."

Part III

Become a Prospecting Machine

CHAPTER 6

BUILDING A TEAM

BECAUSE small and mid-size business have so many opportunities for cross selling, you need to have a team of experts at your command. If your broker-dealer has the resources, you already have the experts to back you up–you just need to introduce yourself to them. You'll need specialists in investments, insurance, banking, investment banking or venture capital, estate planning, etc. These people can be an incredible help to you. Find them, ask to get to know them, and brainstorm with them how to market to business owners in your chosen market. For example, if you talk with a prospect about cash management and you get a bank statement for your expert to analyze, they'll give you a full report on how much money you can either save or make for that prospect. Then you're prepared for your follow-up meeting with the prospect. For each of these experts, ask them how long it takes them to turn around the analysis. If they say one week, tell your prospect that you'll have the analysis completed in about two weeks so that you'll have the analysis in your hands well before your appointment.

Another advantage to assembling the team of experts is that they truly are going to be experts. You don't have go through years of training in order to gain the expertise you want before you start marketing. They've built up the knowledge and skills for you, and they keep up with the industry trends. Once you are on the expert's radar, they'll gladly provide you with hot issues and marketing material, which immediately becomes part of your monthly contact campaign. Finally, they save you time by performing analyses for you.

I once prospected a large engineering firm for years. I got close, but the CFO told me flat out that it would be years before I'd even get a shot at an appointment with him. Then I changed firms, from one wire-house to another. My new employer had a group of experts in using commodities (specifically energy contracts) to hedge against adverse fuel price fluctuations. Like Southwest has always done. I added the trading group to my team, they gave me the talking points for my pitch, and then I called the engineering firm's CFO. As soon as I ran through the talking points, he was hooked. I had an appointment with him the following week. My expert attended and did all the heavy lifting. The prospects CFO was hooked and we presented to the board two months later. Done deal! During one call early on with the CFO, I told him that if we met, he'd find that my team and I are not just a bunch of "me too" guys, all show and no go. After the first meeting, the CFO asked me if I remembered that statement. Then he said that I proved to him that I mean what I say and that I could call him any time with other ideas that would help his company. Bingo! The team of experts approach proved itself again.

Disadvantages? There are none. Period. So build your team of experts. As you gain team members, create an org chart for your team. When you meet with prospects, show them the breadth and depth of your team's expertise. That will set you apart from most other FAs out there.

CHAPTER 7

THE APPOINTMENT

Most rookie FAs waste too much time. Period. They especially waste too much time preparing for meetings with prospects. They'll waste hours preparing proposals that will never be considered, investment recommendations that will not be paid for, and treating the prospect like a client. If you give the prospect a specific proposal before they give you their money to manage, you are working for free. I learned that lesson very early on. I learned it the hard way.

7.1 Don't Work for Free

New FAs will sometimes get "suckered" into giving away their work for free. There are people out there who will prey on the young, eager and naive FAs who will do practically anything to get a client. Consider a conversation such as:

Peter Prospect: "Sure, I'd love to meet with you. I'm not really happy with how my portfolio is doing. You seem like you're smart, so if you can show me that you have some good ideas, I'd be happy to let you manage the account."

FA: (salivating!) "Great. We've already talked a bit about your goals and concerns so I can put together some general ideas that we can refine if you become a client."

PP: "Well, FA, the general ideas are nice, but if you're going to tell me that my existing investments are not the best, you have to tell me why they're not the best, and specifically what you would replace them with, and why. Otherwise I can't really tell that you're any better than my current FA."

Now PP has worked you into a corner. You have to give him specifics. So you spend hours researching individual stocks, etc., and creating proposals for him. Then you meet with PP.

PP: "Why don't you like XYZ Corp as an investment? What do you like better? Oh, ABC Corp? Why do you like it better? Is it the best in its sector?"

You've been had. You've given PP free investment advice, and now the prospect's story changes from "Let's get this portfolio in shape, ASAP," to "This is a big decision and I need to talk with my wife Polly but we'll get back to you after our vacation." Then he starts ducking your phone calls. Sorry, he has a self-service brokerage account, and every so often he suckers another FA to give him new stock tips.

Think about doctors, lawyers or CPAs. How would these next few questions be answered? "Well, doc, why don't you take off two of these moles and then I'll know whether to let you do the other surgery?" Or, asking the lawyer, "How about you represent me for free on this, and then if I see that you're good, I'll hire you for all my other legal work?" Or try to bargain with a CPA, "I want you to do my taxes for free and if I don't get audited I'll hire you next year." If you were lucky, they'd laugh as they escorted you to the door. Why are we different? Why do we have to give it away for free? We don't. So don't!

7.2 Before the Appointment

Newbies also spend a lot of time leading up to the appointment, from spending time prospecting the gate keeper, to spending time preparing the same presentation over and over again.

Dealing with the "Gate Keeper"

Some FAs (okay, *most* FAs) hate the gatekeeper (the receptionist, the personal secretary, etc.) In many cases, you can avoid the gatekeepers altogether by calling when they are not available, early in the morning before they get into the office, during lunch hour, or after they leave in the afternoon. Many business owners will get into the office at 7:00am, not take lunch, and stay well into the evening. Call at those times. I'm a big believer in breakfast (or morning coffee) meetings, and on days when you don't have such a face-to-face meeting scheduled, make additional phone calls then.

At other times, face it, you'll talk to gatekeepers. Some advisors hang up as soon as they get the receptionist or the owner's secretary. I think that this is a mistake. Turn the gatekeeper into one of your allies. Let her or him know that (i) you are different than all of those other advisors who call every day (and back it up, don't just make bald claims); (ii) all you really want to do is to see if you can help; and (iii) if you cannot help, you won't bother them again.

Schiffman's and Mattson's books (each listed in the "Resources" chapter) contains specific tactics. Study them, practice them, and use them.

One question that you have to answer is, "Who is really the gatekeeper and who is really the decision maker?" A decent small business will have a CFO and the receptionist may tell you that the CFO is the proper person for you to talk. Resist that. If you begin your discussions with the CFO, that person becomes gatekeeper number two. Also, you are looking to break up an existing relationship. The CFO may be waiting for the chance to offer the business to, for example, his son-in-law. You coming into the picture creates such an opportunity. Another strategic thought is which carries more weight, the CFO making a recommendation to his/her boss, or the CFO's boss making a "recommendation" to the CFO. So work from the top of the organizational chart down. You'll have a better chance of success.

Prepare a "Universal Pitch Book"

Do this before you go into production so you don't spend valuable prospecting time on it. If you're already in production, do this in the evenings or on the weekends. As you build the pitch book, remember that everything that you do must convey professionalism and quality. Don't skimp or do anything slipshod.

Buy a high-quality three-ring binder, and a set of dividers. Go to your favorite big-box office supply store and browse the aisles. There are some very nice sets available that has plastic front and back pieces (so your pages don't curl around the binder's rings), and plastic tabbed dividers for each section. They come in different sets, some with five dividers, others with eight, etc. So plan out your sections before you go shopping. At a minimum, you might want one divider for individual prospects and a second for businesses. The personal pitch book might include the following sections:

- About us (your virtual team's org chart and possibly a quick biography of the team members).
- About (wire-house name): Your broker-dealer probably already has a piece addressing this.
- Financial planning
- Investments: Break this down as you see fit. You might include managed money programs, for example.
- Alternative investments
- Insurance
- Retirement Income Solutions
- Banking and lending

A business-oriented pitch book would be more comprehensive and might include:

- About us (see above)
- About my company (see above)
- Cash management
- Investments
- Insurance

- Buy/sell funding
- Qualified retirement plans
- Non-qualified plans & executive compensation plans

Assuming that your firm's marketing pieces are all letter sized, you can simply three-hole punch them and put them into the binder. Create a nice table of contents using the template provided by the divider manufacturer, and you're ready to go. If you can, work with your team members to create sample case studies and put those in the appropriate section. This gives you the ability to show the prospect what you (your firm) have done for your prospect's competitors. That's much more impressive and convincing than a pitch filled with empty promises. Compliance has some very specific rules dealing with case studies, so check with them first, and then tailor your approach to keep compliance happy.

Now you have one pitch book for every prospect meeting and you don't have to spend time pulling marketing material off of the computer as you're getting ready to run out to meet the prospect. Next step, work out a "script" for a short pitch about each tab. Remember that telling is not selling, so don't give them speeches. I've heard rookies talking about how great their firm is. You only need to do that if your b-d doesn't advertise or is not a household name. I used to tell prospects, "I could spend about six and a half hours telling you about everything that my firm does. But I don't want to put you to sleep. You know my firm, right? (They acknowledge.) If it involves money or making money, we probably do it and we're probably pretty good at it. But do you have any specific questions about my firm?"

7.3 During the Appointment

Your sole goal is to add value to your future clients' lives. You are there to help them. That must be your mindset. Some pointers are:

Ask about their businesses in general. If appropriate, ask for a tour. They've worked long and hard to build their businesses and would probably be flattered you asked and proud to show you around. It will also help you learn more about the industry.

Ask a lot of specific questions: How have you handled the recession? How many minimum-wage employees do you have and how would raising it affect you? How are you dealing with the new healthcare requirements? (Note: Do not get into a political discussion–you don't care about politics. You care only about how the existing laws affect your clients.) The financial crisis and recession have impacted many companies' banking relationships. Yours?

Telling is not selling. You should talk maybe 20% of the time and most of that is to ask questions. The other 80% is listening to the prospect or client. Ask a question, listen to the answer, then ask a follow up question.

7.4 After the Appointment

Diligent follow-through is key. If you promise to do something within one week, you damned well better do it within six days, not seven. Put another way, keep every promise. If you can't keep a promise during the sales process, the owner is going to know that you won't keep your promise after you've locked her company in as a client.

Follow through consistently. Set up a schedule. Monthly (at least) contact is necessary. Set a schedule in which you phone the contact monthly and then either drop off or mail useful information to them periodically (perhaps quarterly). The "drop off" is discussed further a few paragraphs down.

Studies have shown that the average person needs to be "asked for the sale" five to seven times before agreeing. Other studies have shown that the average FA stops contacting the prospect after three times. See the inconsistency there? In your initial calls, cull out the jerks and the unqualified, and contact the remaining suspects/prospects once a month like clockwork. You have to keep up the contacts because with each conversation, your chances go up.

7.4. AFTER THE APPOINTMENT

In your monthly contacts, you've got to have something to talk about. Something that is valuable to them. Don't call them once a month and just say something self-serving like, "Hi this is Dana from XYZ financial. I'm just calling again to see if you'd like to sit down and discuss how we can help you." How about, "Hi this is Dana from XYZ Financial and a lot of people in your industry have been concerned about [insert topic]. If you'd like to hear about what your competitors are doing to resolve that issue, I'd be glad to sit down with you."

Another good tactic is to "drop in on your way to work" with some pertinent information. I put that in quotes because that's what you'll tell the owner: "I put together this information on [important issue] and I decided to drop it off to save the mailing delay." A few important points: (i) it must actually be timely, time-sensitive, and important (worth you taking the time to drop it off personally); (ii) there's a decent chance that if you took the time to drop something off, the owner will at the very least say hello and shake your hand; and (iii) even if that happens, don't force your way into an unscheduled appointment–tell the owner that you appreciate the offer but you don't want to interrupt his/her schedule, and that you'll call in a week to see if he/she has any questions on it. Your consideration will win you points.

For a few reasons, you can't drop off information to all of your contacts every single month. First, it would take too much time. Second, it's disingenuous. Their office can't always be "on the way" and not everything can be that time sensitive. For most of these informative contacts, mail the information. Save the "drop off" for very important or time-sensitive pieces. And remember that your compliance department has to review every piece that you deliver to a prospect or client. And just on a practical side, mailing things simply wastes time because prospects don't read most of what you send them anyway. At best, it goes into the "read later" pile. You're better off just calling them.

CHAPTER 8

TIME MANAGEMENT → SUCCESS

TIME management is crucial. How much discipline you either have or develop will have probably the biggest impact on whether you succeed or fail in this business. That's not to say that if you manage your time, you are guaranteed to succeed. Rather, if you cannot manage your time you are fighting an uphill battle.

8.1 An Illustrative Tale

Let me describe a typical morning. It's 8:00 a.m., and two FAs walk into their office building. As they ride up the elevator, they chat.

John: "Hey, Karen. Busy day today?"
Karen: "Yeah, I had two appointments yesterday afternoon, and got one account."
John: "Wow, good job! So you'll be doing the paperwork today?"
Karen: No, I came back into the office last night and got everything ready to hand to my assistant. So I shouldn't have anything to do on it today."
John: "But you said you're busy today?"
Karen: "Yeah, I still need to make 200 dials today."
John: "Yeah, I've got to make some calls today, too."

The elevator gets to their floor. As soon as Karen sits down at her desk, reviews her to-do list and pulls her calling list from her file drawer. John, on the other hand, logs in and checks his favorite news and sports websites.

By 8:15, Karen is calling. John is still reading his news and emailing his friends. Other FAs start filtering into the office. They all see Karen on the phone so they don't interrupt her work. John makes sure that he says "hello" to all of them and starts a conversation whenever he can. John rationalizes it because it's the first thing in the morning and he needs to "warm up his voice" and let the coffee kick in. Then around 10:00 he decides to see what's happening in the markets so he'll have something to talk about when he does start calling. After all, it will only take a couple of minutes, right? Another FA stops by John's cubicle and they chat about the markets and what to say to a prospect in response to some crazy objection that will most likely never come up again. Then, John sees that cute little intern he's been admiring and he can't pass up the chance to talk with her. When she's done, John's clock says 11:30 and he thinks, "Well, I can't start calling now. All my prospects are probably trying to get things wrapped up so they can go out to lunch. So I'm going to take my lunch break and maybe go to the gym." Meanwhile, Karen is still calling.

In the afternoon, John's excuses continue. Right after lunch, he feels that a prospect probably has to answer all of those lunch time voice mails, so he'll wait until 2:00 to start calling "again." Even the, he decides that he'll call only for an hour or two because the prospects are probably trying to wrap things up so they can get out of the office before rush hour begins. One of John's buddies sends him a text about some infuriating thing that Congress is doing or something about the upcoming election. John is very political, so they argue until 3:30. Now John decides that he'll research for the rest of the day and then start calling "for real" first thing the next morning. Unfortunately, John said the same thing at least three days of every week for the last few months. That is his pattern.

Fast forward a year. Karen has graduated early from the training program and has increased her revenue enough that she's earned an office. John asked her how she did it and she replied simply: "You remember all of those mornings when we came into the office first thing and we both said that we needed to prospect? Well I sat down and started dialing. I gave myself a daily quota of dials–a morning quota and an afternoon quota. No news, no internet, no email, no talking until I hit my morning quota. That's the difference."

That story is true, but I've changed the names. Karen represents about 8 out of 100 rookies and John represents the other 92.

Karen can teach us many valuable lessons, from planning your week in advance to reviewing and rewarding your accomplishments every single day.

8.2 Scheduling and Chunking

The most important thing you can do to successfully manage your time is to create a schedule and stick to it. We've already discussed created a model weekly schedule. The unsuccessful advisors that I've seen had their priorities backwards. Everyone avoids cold calling because it's uncomfortable. So new FAs will do almost anything else on their to-do list before saying, "Well, I guess I have to make some calls now." Flip that attitude. You know how many hours per week you need to call, so block them off on your schedule. After prospecting is blocked out on your schedule, "client service" is the next most important task. But that's flexible because you can control when and where it happens.

8.3 Managing Appointments

Are you a professional? Like a doctor or a lawyer? I hope the answer is in the affirmative. So start thinking like a doctor. Stop making house calls. Get your clients in the mindset that they are going to come to your office for their periodic checkups. Train them to do that from the beginning. How long would it take to drive to the client's office or home? Add an hour or two meeting the client, and then another drive back to your office? Compare that to just having them meet you at your office. There's no decision. Yes, you have to meet with people during prospecting, but after they are your client, you have to set the ground rules.

When you meet with prospects and clients, use an agenda. Use the same agenda for all similar meetings. Put times on the agenda. Five minutes for the warmup. Ten minutes for this and fifteen minutes for that. You can help to control the time by setting expectations at the beginning. Here's a typical conversation:

Fred FA (FA): "Ms. Prospect, thanks for taking the time to meet with me."

Pat Prospect (PP): "No problem, thanks for coming to my office so early in the morning."

FA: "You're welcome. I know you're busy, and I need to leave in an hour at the latest, so I put together this agenda about what I thought would be good to discuss. Is there anything you'd like to add to the agenda?"

PP: "Actually, the biggest question I have is [questions and concerns]. That's the one that keeps me up at night."

FA: "Thanks for mentioning it. Let's talk about that here [point to an appropriate spot on the agenda and then write the prospect's topic on the page]."

Now you've set a time limit, created a road map for the meeting, and found out the prospect's biggest concern. That's a pretty good accomplishment for the first five minutes of a meeting.

If you call businesses, the gatekeepers generally leave the office at a predictable time, but that time may depend on the specific industry. You should have that time figured out within your first week dialing. Once the gatekeeper leaves, that usually opens up another window of phone calls. You may want to stay "late" a few times a week so you can take advantage of that. If so, in the late afternoon, take a break from calling so you can be refreshed for your round of calls in the early evening.

8.4 Productivity Tips

In the Mornings

<++>

- → Get to the office on time, and set a specific time that you will pick up the phone.
- → Don't feel the need to "warm up the voice." It took me a year to realize that the first few cold calls are not going to be that great. But those first few calls will warm up the voice.
- → When your schedule says you need to start calling, pick up the phone and dial the next number on your list. Just do it. The first call is the hardest, so don't even think about it. Just make the call. The second one comes naturally.

Lunchtime

- → Don't eat with your coworkers unless there's a good reason to do so. A valid business reason. If you're not having lunch discussing business, and by that I mean you have a legitimate expectation of either gaining a client or somehow leading you closer to prospects or clients, then don't do it. Lunches should make you better: They should give you an afternoon's energy and make you better somehow, either financially or in terms of skills.
- → During lunch, unless you're meeting clients or prospects for lunch, get away from the office. Even if it's just to walk a few blocks. It will rejuvenate you for the afternoon's work.
- → Use lunches efficiently. I knew one advisor who would schedule two back-to-back lunches with two different prospects. At 11:30, he'd have an early lunch with one prospect, then at 1:00 he'd have a late lunch with a second prospect. He picked either the same restaurant or two restaurants near each other, and made sure that they had healthy food. At one of the lunches,

he'd eat only a salad. At the other, he might have soup and a half sandwich. In other words, he had two light lunches, watched the nutritional content. He didn't tell either prospect that he was doing another lunch, but if anyone saw him and said anything he'd just tell them that it was more convenient for the client that way. Between the two lunches, he returned the phone calls that he missed in the morning.

Shutting Down for the Evening

- → When you begin to wind down from calling for the day, review your "to do" list for today to ensure you've done everything. Then make a task list for tomorrow.
- → Clean your desk. Get everything off of your desk that doesn't need to be there. All papers should be processed or filed. In other words, get them off of your desk. All the research shows that having papers on the desk reduces your productivity.
- → When you finally finish your calls, one last time make sure that you've returned all calls and messages, then go home. Now that you know that you've taken care of everything today and have tomorrow all planned out, you can relax, enjoy the evening, and sleep well.

General Productivity Tips

- → For each hour you have blocked off for dialing, stick to it. Maybe you call for 50 minutes and surf the net for ten minutes. After the next 50 minutes, you run to get a coffee.
- → You've already put your goals on paper, right? Yearly goals, quarterly, monthly, weekly, daily, and hourly. The yearly and quarterly goals will be asset and revenue targets. The monthly, weekly, daily and hourly goals will be activity goals. If you want to make $XXX,000 in revenue, you need to make 4,000 dials per month. That's 1,000 per week or 200 per day. If

8.4. PRODUCTIVITY TIPS

you can make 50 dials per hour, that's four hours of dialing, so you might schedule calling from 9:00 to 11:30 for dialing (including a little break), and then another two hours of dialing in the afternoon.

→ Set up little rewards for yourself. When I was a trainee, I went through my business plan with my wife. We set up rewards if I hit my activity goals. Daily activity goals–I got dessert. Weekly activity–a martini and a movie on Friday evening. Set one appointment in a day, I didn't have to help with the dishes after dinner. Set two appointments in one day, a back rub. My wife thought that she'd be funny, so she wrote down a reward for what I'd get if I set three appointments in one day. I won't tell you what it was, so I suppose you can guess the general topic. But it was a nice reward and I was happy when I won it!

→ From your business plan, take next year's salary target and divide that number by 2,000. That is how much your time is worth per hour. If you can pay someone to do any task worth less than that per hour then you should pay them to do it so that you can focus on production. Caveats: If you're just going to sit around and watch TV, it's a losing proposition. It only works if you actually work (either prospecting or client service) while you're paying them to clean your house, for example.

→ Dealing with incoming phone calls. While you're making calls, don't answer the phone. If you have an assistant, talk with her/him (sorry, most are females even nowadays) about how to handle incoming calls for you. My system was that my CA would take down the caller's name, phone number, and whether the call was time sensitive, and then if the caller wanted to leave more detail, she put him into voice mail. She wrote the basic information onto one of those little pink message forms and put it in front of me on my desk. Then, at lunch time, I could grab all of the slips and walk out to lunch and return the calls as I walked or as I waited at the restaurant.

→ Incorporating prospecting into your day is an exercise in time chunking and scheduling. If you decide to call businesses and you want to call them between 7:30am and 9:00am, without fail, because that's before the gatekeeper is in, then you need to make that 90 minute time frame sacrosanct. Don't schedule appointments with anyone during that time. And be sure that you pick up the phone and dial a number from your list as soon as the clock hits 7:30.

Appendices

THE FA'S BUSINESS PLAN TEMPLATE

A typical business plan (like the templates you'll find on the Small Business Administration website) is more comprehensive than an FA needs. For your purposes, the plan covers only a few areas: (i) your business niche(s); (ii) current revenue and future revenue goals; and (iii) your marketing plan. You can also add a fourth section on professional development. Start with the outline below, and then incorporate all of the exercises and elements from this book.

I. My business and niches:
  a. Small businesses
    → industry
    → minimum and maximum revenue
    → profitability
    → privately-owned
    → geographic limitations
  b. CPAs (marketing to CPAs is discussed in my companion book)
  c. THIRD NICHE etc.
II. Revenue goals
  a. Current revenue
  b. Future revenue
    → Quarterly targets for the first two to five years, then annually thereafter.
    → Your revenue targets should exceed your employer's minimums.
    → Sub-total revenue, if you can, into sub-totals from managed money, transactional, insurance, etc. If not, don't

worry about it, just assume 100% managed money and treat any transactions as a "bonus."

III. Marketing
   a. General
      → How many hours per week will you prospect?
      → How will you prospect? Which methods? How many hours per week?
      → Include your weekly schedule template with the three categories: client acquisition; client service; and other.
      → Block off "standard meeting times"
      → Show breakfast appointment slots and lunch appointment slots, etc.
   b. Small business prospecting
      → Show cold-calling hours, hours of networking (don't disclose actual events, etc., because that's *your* business), seminar slots, etc.
      → Show numbers of calls needed, and when those calls will be made.
      → Include your calling ratios for reference.
   c. Include similar items for each chosen market niche.
IV. Professional Development: List all professional development courses and seminars you'd like to attend. I'd highly recommend further sales training. The only training I would suggest though is Sandler Sales training. The investment will pay off. (Please note that I have no financial interest in Sandler Sales or in any of its franchisees–this recommendation is because it works. Period.

ADDITIONAL RESOURCES

As I mentioned before, I've read practically every book related to the business aspects of being an FA. The following is a list of the books that I found to be particularly helpful.

General Marketing and Selling

- Thomas J. Stanley, PhD, *The Millionaire Next Door*
- Stanley, *Marketing to the Affluent*
- Stanley, *Networking with the Affluent*
- Stanley, *Selling to the Affluent*

Networking

- Susan RoAne, *How To Work a Room* (very high level discussion)
- Ivan Misner, *The 29% Solution: 52 Weekly Networking Success Stories*
- Dale Carnegie Training. *See* www.DaleCarnegie.com for more information.

Cold-Calling

- Stephan Schiffman, *Cold Calling Techniques (That Really Work)*
- David Mattson, *Five Minutes with VITO*

Seminars

- Frank Maselli, Seminars: *Seminars: The Emotional Dynamic*. The book is apparently not currently in print, but there seem to be plenty of new and used copies available on Amazon through third-party sellers. Wholesalers used to give this book away a lot, so you might want to ask your wholesalers if their office has any extra copies lying around.

Goals and Motivation

- Napoleon Hill, *Think and Grow Rich* This book is the foundation for all others.
- Zig Ziglar, *Born to Win* I'd suggest this in print (paper or Kindle) and on audio. It's great to listen to on a morning run or on the way to work.
- Brian Tracy, *Goals*
- Denis Waitley, *Psychology of Winning* This another work that is fantastic on audio, and is good for the morning workout or commute. Waitley is a great speaker.

Time Management

- Brian Tracy, *Time Management*
- Brian Tracy, *Eat that Frog!*
- The best resource (in my humble opinion) is my forthcoming book, Time Management for FAs, which will be published in March 2014. (I'd apologize for the shameless self-promotion, but self-promotion is a great quality to have. You should learn it, too!)

Learning about Businesses

– John A. Tracy, *How To Read a Financial Report*: I strongly recommend this book because when your business-owner prospects or clients talk about "gross," "net," "SG&A," or "EBITDA," you ought to know what they mean.

www.ingramcontent.com/pod-product-compliance
Lightning Source LLC
Chambersburg PA
CBHW051815170526
45167CB00005B/2017